The angels are getting ready to announce the birth of the Christ child.

Each angel has a role. Some sing in the choir. Others guide the shepherds by telling them about the baby in the manger.

...and then there is Xavier.

The Angels Birthday Celebration

Coloring Pages Inside

Joyce Carr Stedelbauer

HighTide
Publications, Inc.

Deltaville, Virginia

Luke 2:1-20 New International Version (NIV)

The Birth of Jesus

2 In those days Caesar Augustus issued a decree that a census should be taken of the entire Roman world. 2 (This was the first census that took place while Quirinius was governor of Syria.) 3 And everyone went to their own town to register.

4 So Joseph also went up from the town of Nazareth in Galilee to Judea, to Bethlehem the town of David, because he belonged to the house and line of David. 5 He went there to register with Mary, who was pledged to be married to him and was expecting a child. 6 While they were there, the time came for the baby to be born, 7 and she gave birth to her firstborn, a son. She wrapped him in cloths and placed him in a manger, because there was no guest room available for them.

8 And there were shepherds living out in the fields nearby, keeping watch over their flocks at night. 9 An angel of the Lord appeared to them, and the glory of the Lord shone around them, and they were terrified. 10 But the angel said to them, "Do not be afraid. I bring you good news that will cause great joy for all the people. 11 Today in the town of David a Savior has been born to you; he is the Messiah, the Lord. 12 This will be a sign to you: You will find a baby wrapped in cloths and lying in a manger."

13 Suddenly a great company of the heavenly host appeared with the angel, praising God and saying,

14 "Glory to God in the highest heaven, and on earth peace to those on whom his favor rests."

15 When the angels had left them and gone into heaven, the shepherds said to one another, "Let's go to Bethlehem and see this thing that has happened, which the Lord has told us about."

16 So they hurried off and found Mary and Joseph, and the baby, who was lying in the manger. 17 When they had seen him, they spread the word concerning what had been told them about this child, 18 and all who heard it were amazed at what the shepherds said to them. 19 But Mary treasured up all these things and pondered them in her heart. 20 The shepherds returned, glorifying and praising God for all the things they had heard and seen, which were just as they had been told.

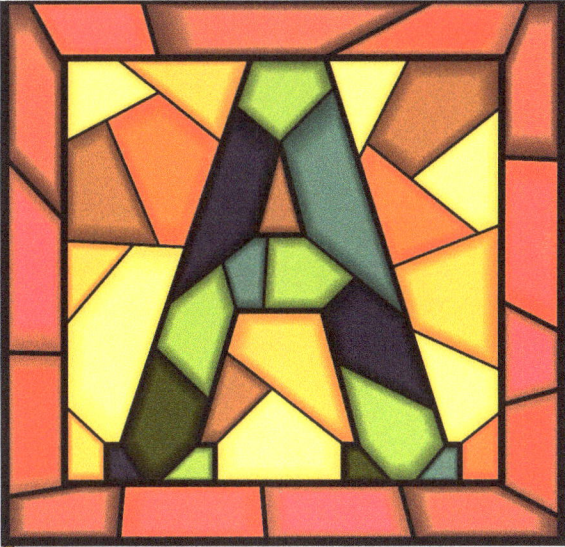

Angels

Angels almost always sing on key---
except Xavier.

Bells

Beautiful bells ring joyful news over Bethlehem proclaiming the Baby's birth.

Choirs

Cherub choirs at the church concentrate on Christmas carols to bless all the earth.

Dancing

Dancing stars practice routines to dazzle a dark
sky that is
higher than high,

Evensong

Evensong practice 3 p.m. Where's Xavier? He sings a little flat and is in danger of sky-diving split-splat.

Forever

Forever late is not a familiar problem for most Angels but Xavier sometimes misses all the fun.

Gowns

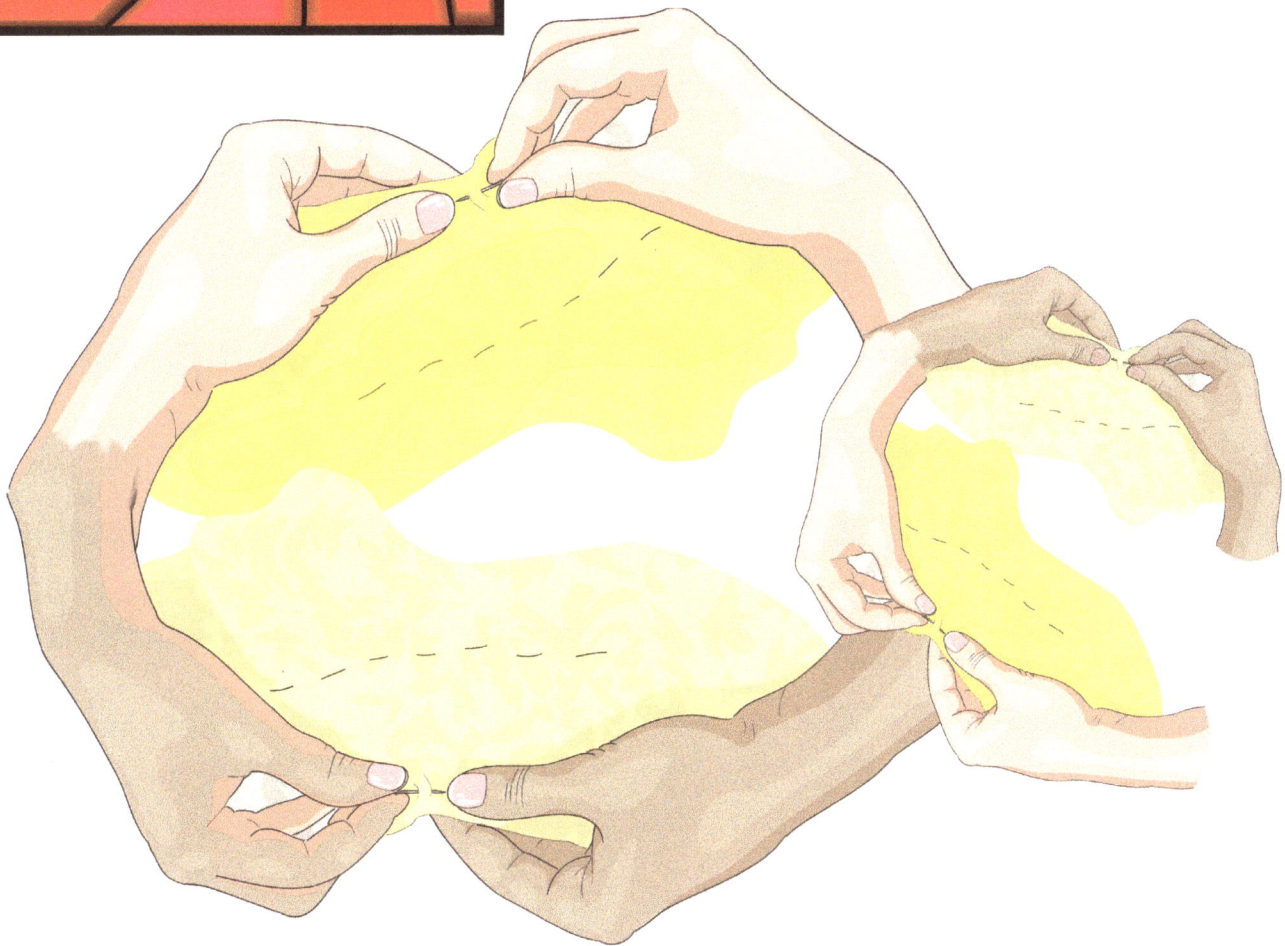

Golden gowns are ordered
for the great choir
to glow like the gleaming sun.

Hosts

Heavenly Hosts of Angels sing Hallelujah, Hosanna in the Highest, Hallelujah!

Immanuel

Immanuel, God with us.
How can it be? Where is Xavier?
Come and see!

Jesus

Jesus, said the Angel Gabriel,
is the Baby's Name.
We are full of joy that He came.

Kings

Kings will bow their knees, bringing gifts,
singing hymns,
at the mention of His Name.

Lord

Lord Jesus, Lamb of God, is it really true that you love everyone? Even Xavier and me too?

Mary

Mary, Jesus' Mother, sang her majestic Magnificat to tell us yes, God loves us.

Noel

NOEL   NOEL   NOEL

Noel, Noel, the Choir knows what Christmas is for, God has a welcome wreath on His door.

Open

8 And there were shepherds living out in the fields nearby, keeping watch over their flocks at night. 9 An angel of the Lord appeared to them, and the glory of the Lord shone around them, and they were terrified. 10 But the angel said to them, "Do not be afraid. I bring you good news that will cause great joy for all the people. 11 Today in the town of David a Savior has been born to you; he is the Messiah, the Lord. 12 This will be a sign to you: You will find a baby wrapped in cloths and lying in a manger."

13 Suddenly a great company of the heavenly host appeared with the angel, praising God and saying,

14 "Glory to God in the highest heaven, and on earth peace to those on whom his favor rests."

My Bible

Only the ones who open the Bible and read and dream and look can find answers in His Book.

Presents

People are making or purchasing presents to present their love gifts around the Christmas Tree.

Quickly

Quickly, the clock keeps us on cue. Tick-Tock, Xavier's behavior is a quirky problem. Tick-Tock

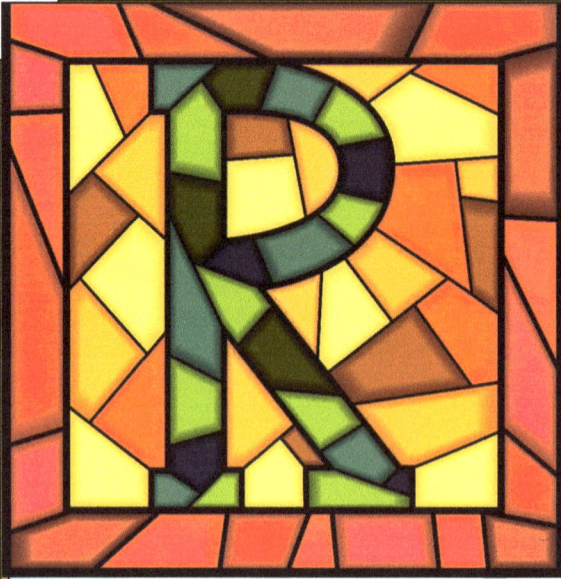

Remarkable

Remember the angels are ready to tell the remarkable story, singing over and over Glory, Glory!

Stars

See, the stars are shining, choirs are singing,
some people on earth are already snoozing.

Time

Xavier

Xavier

1...2...3...4...5...6...7...8...9...10...11...12

Xavier

The appointed time is Midnight.
Please find Xavier!
Tell him that Jesus the Savior is here!

Universe

The Universe is United in readiness for the Christmas celebration!
You will be sorry if you are still sleeping...

Visitors

Visitors and pets are welcome too!

Whoever

Whoever wants to see Christmas glory,
get a blanket,
lie down outside and look up to see...

Xavier

Xavier, in his golden gown, smiling, singing on key and dancing at the edge of high, dark sky.

You

You too, can sing and dance and bring your gift to welcome Baby Jesus on Christmas Day.

Zion

Zion, Mount of Olives,
the Church of all Nations.
Pray for Peace.

About the Author

Joyce Carr Stedelbauer is an award winning poet.

The delight of doing children's books is a long realized dream. The Awesome Alphabet Animal Party was the first, also published by High Tide Publications.

Other books by Joyce Stedelbauer:
- Have You Met Eve?
- Have You Seen the Star?
- Who Rolled the Stone?
- Where Are You Adam?

She is an active member of the National League of American Pen Women and the Poetry Society Of Virginia.

She and her husband George live in Williamsburg Virginia. They enjoye their two children and six grandchildren

1. Are angels real?

     Yes, angels are real, spirit beings.

2. Have you ever seen an angel?

     Yes_____ No_____I'm not sure_____

3. Where did angels come from?

     The Bible explains that angels were created by God.

4. Are angels people who have died and gone to heaven?

     No, people and angels are separate and distinct beings.

5. Where do angels live?

     Angels live in heavenly spaces.

6. What do angels do?

     Angels serve God as messengers. They help provide encouragement and protection.

7. Are all angels good?

     Angels were all created to be good, but some have rebelled against God out of pride.

8. What happened to those angels?

     They chose to serve Lucifer, the first prideful, fallen angel.

9. Can angels do things that humans cannot do?

     Yes, angels can travel throughout the universe on God's orders.

10. Do angels ever come to earth?

     Yes, angels can come to earth on assignment from God.

11. Do angels always wear robes and wings?

     No, angels can appear looking just like us, helping people on earth.

12. Do we have guardian angels?

     Yes, we have more than one angel who cares for us.

13. Are angels beautiful?

     Yes, the Bible gives wonderful details of their shining appearance and clothing.

14. Do angels sing?

     Yes, the Hallelujah chorus is heard many times in many languages all praising God.

15. How many Christmas songs do you know? _____

16. How many angels are there?

     Thousands upon ten-thousands of angels exist.

17. Do we know everything about angels?

     No, only God knows everything.

Can you draw angels making children in the clouds like we make angels in the snow?

Coloring Pages

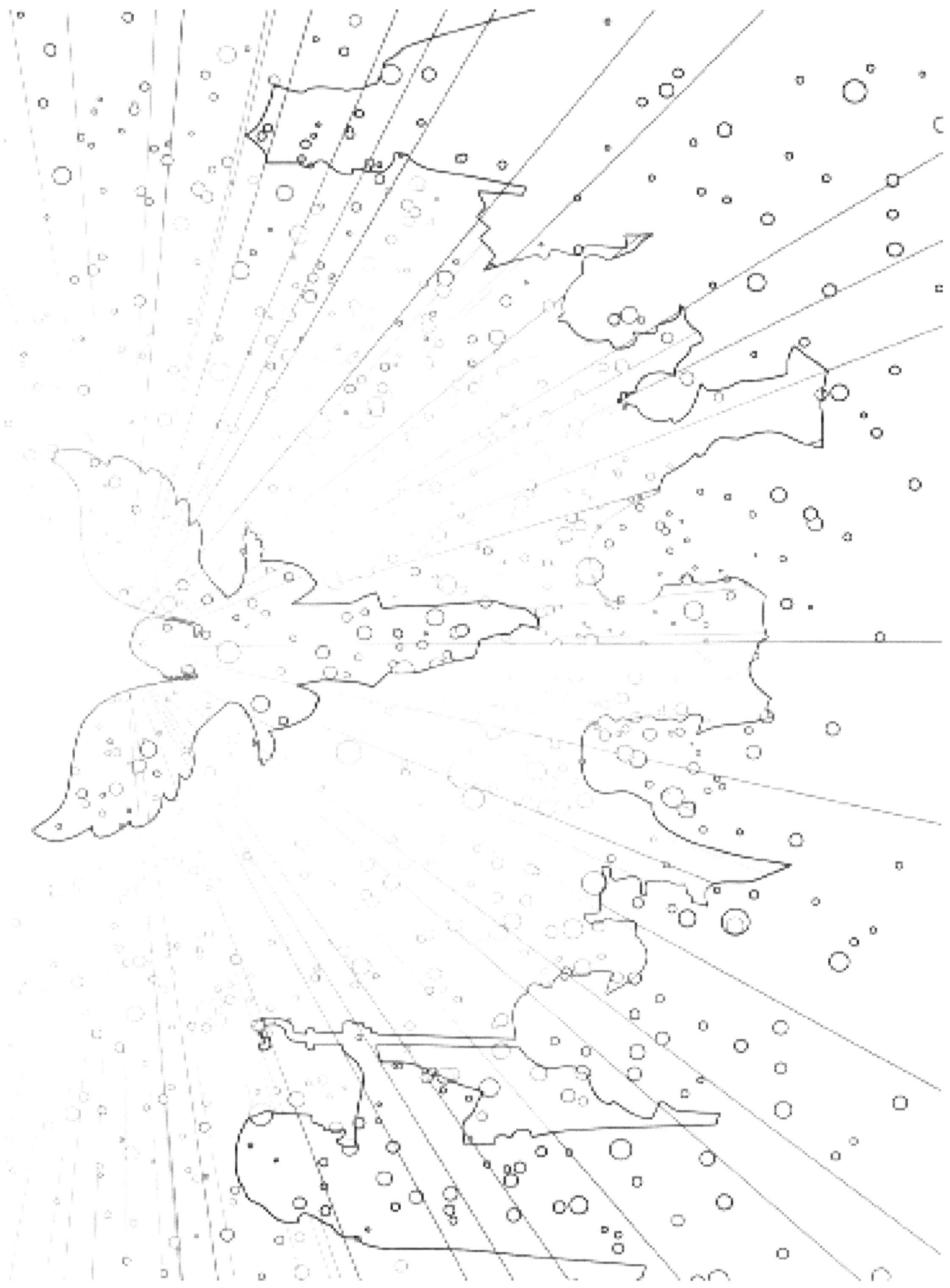

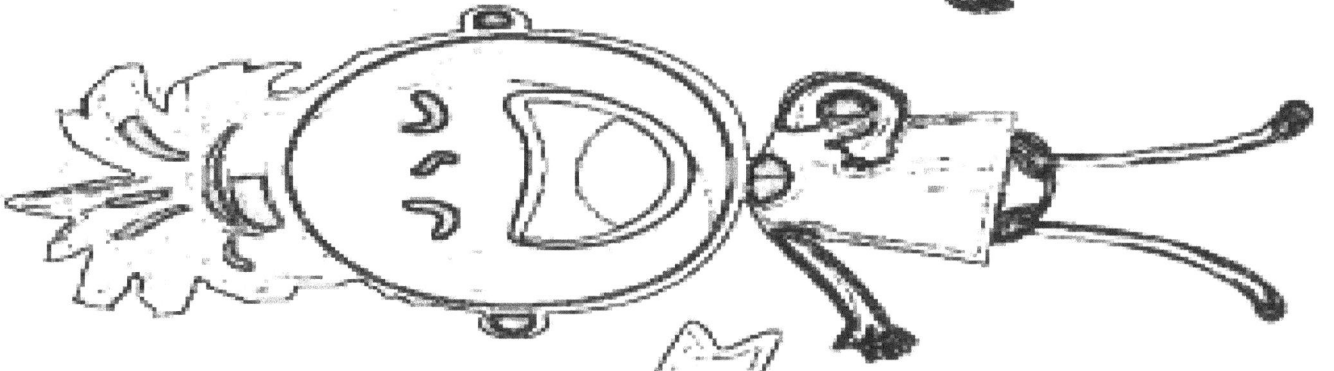

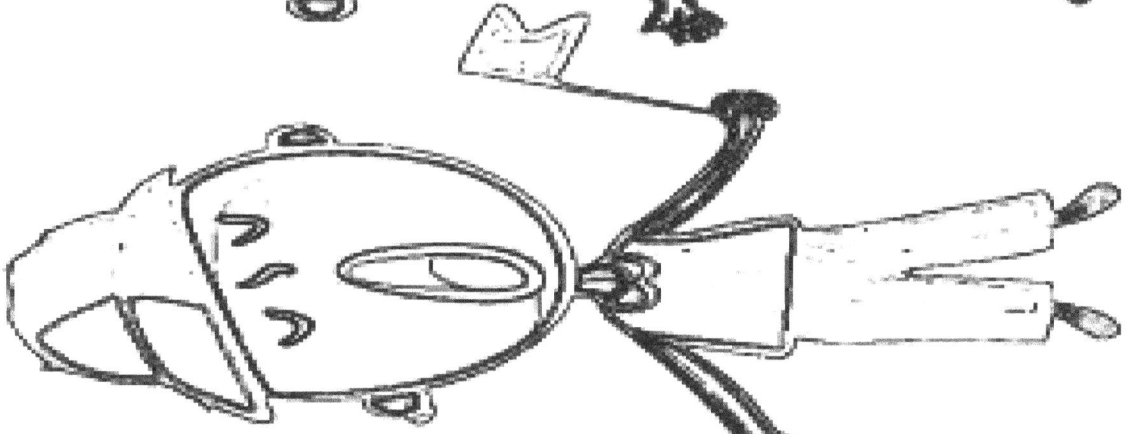

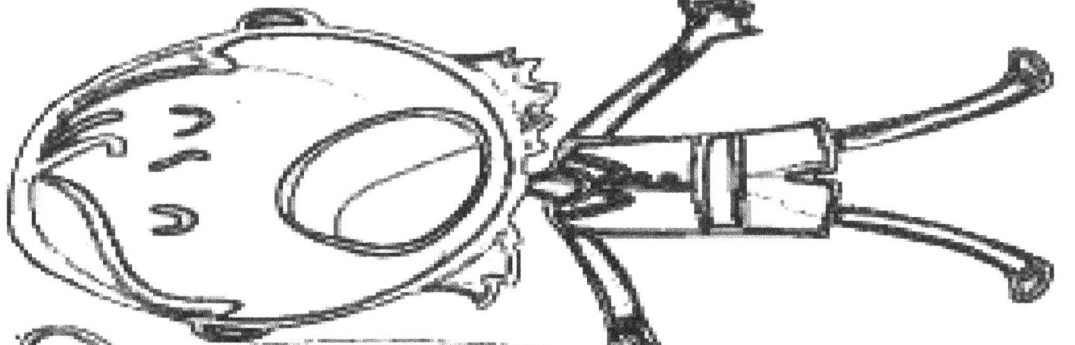

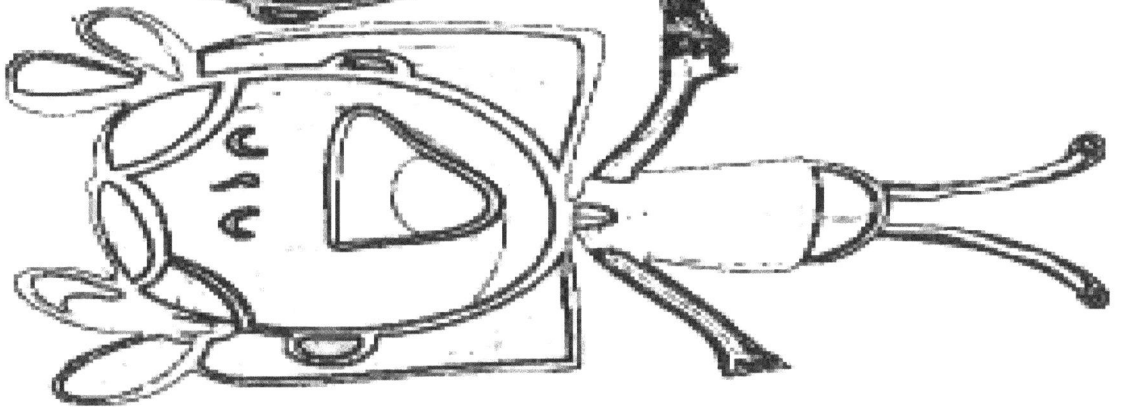

Xavier seems to be missing a few things.

Can you draw his face, his halo, and his wings?

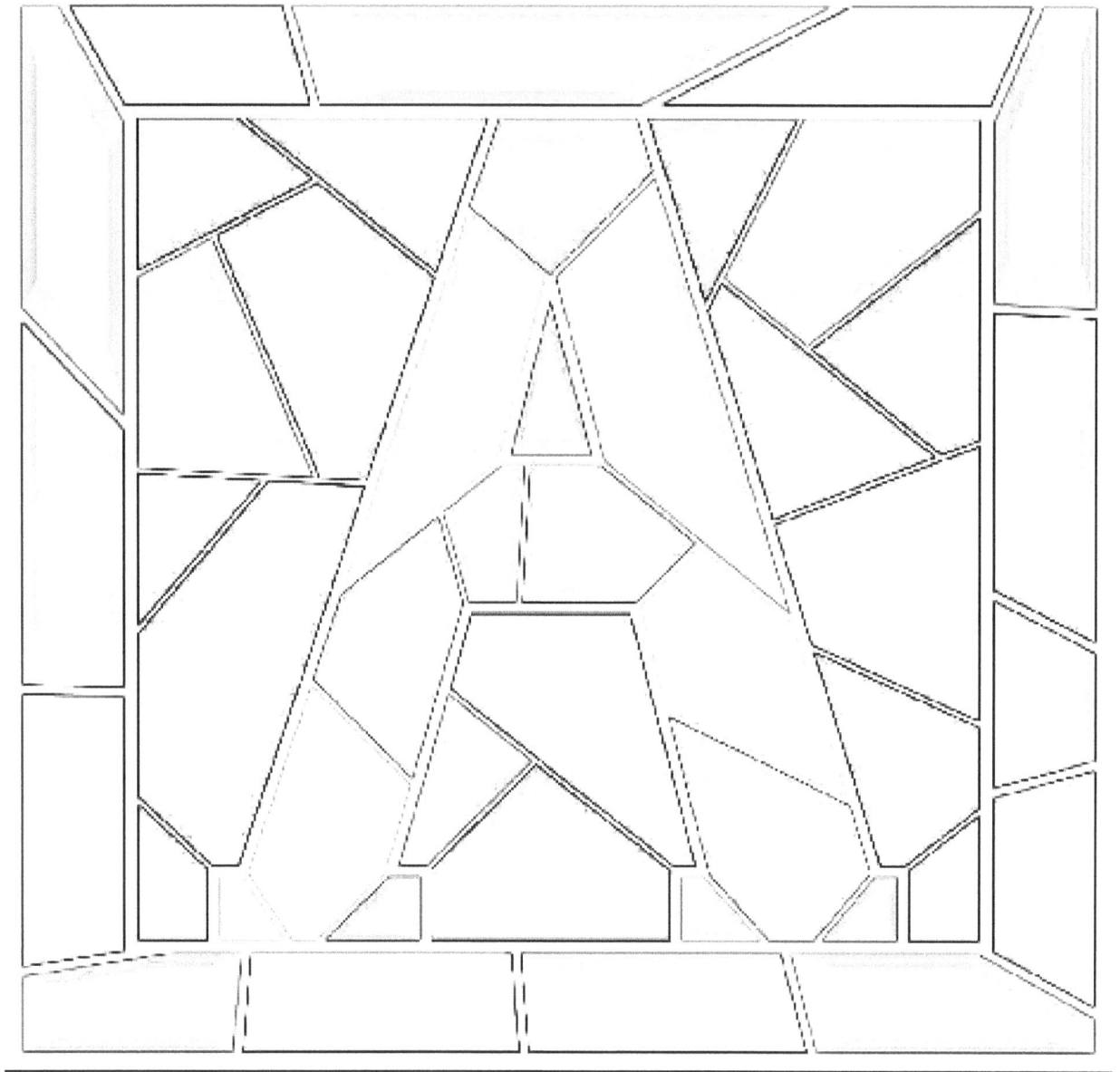

A is for
Angel

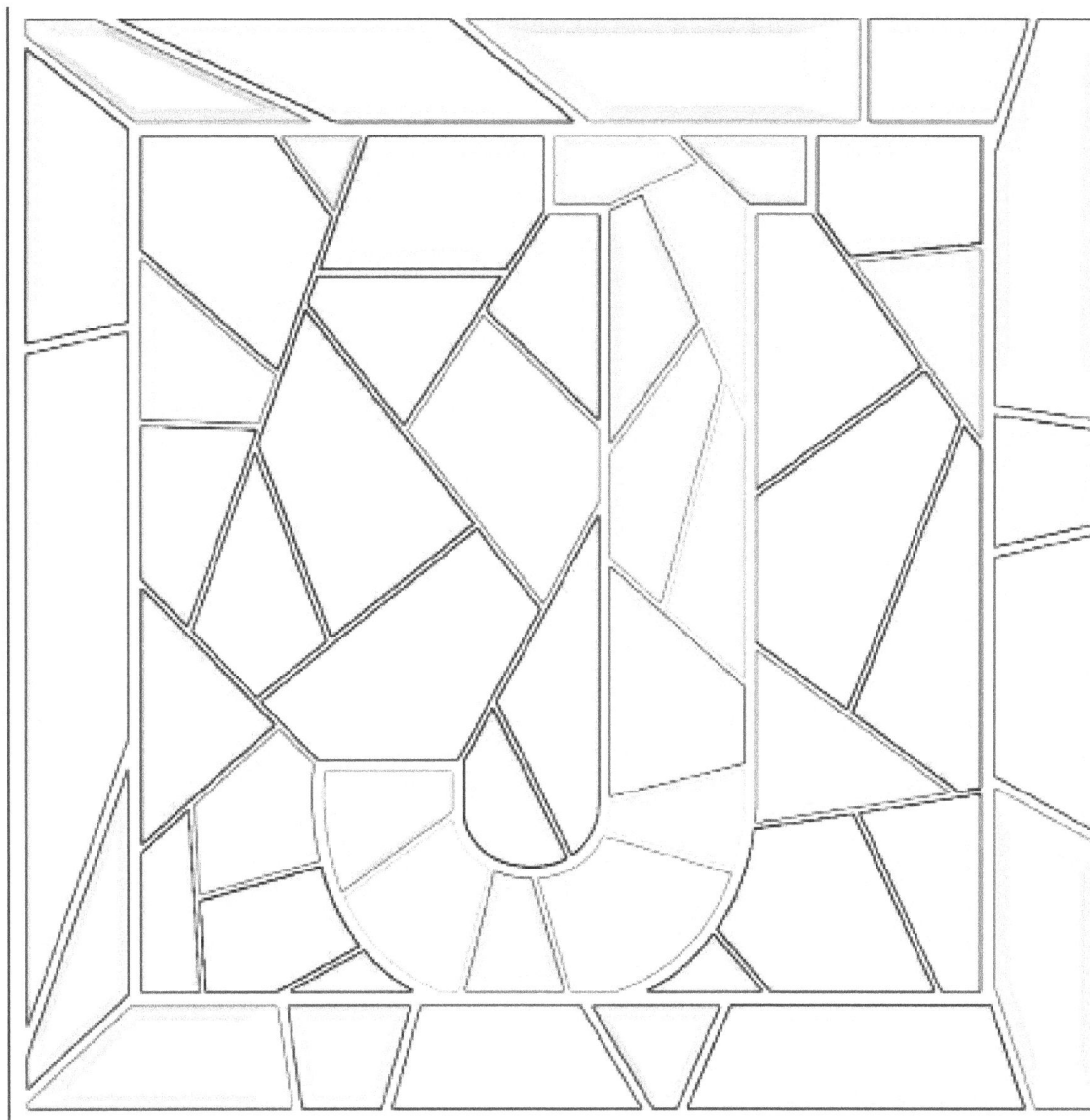

J is for

Jesus

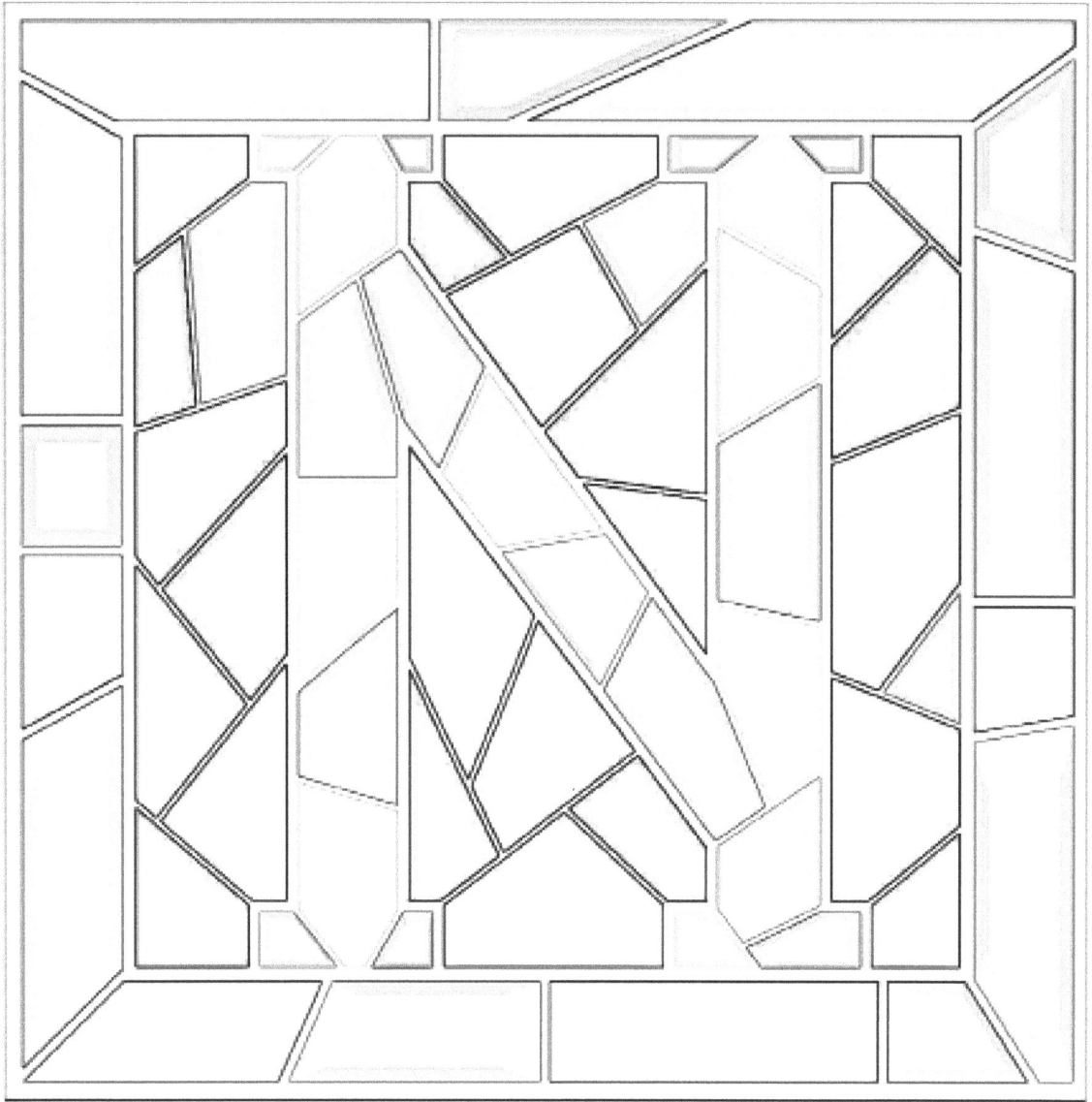

N is for
Noel

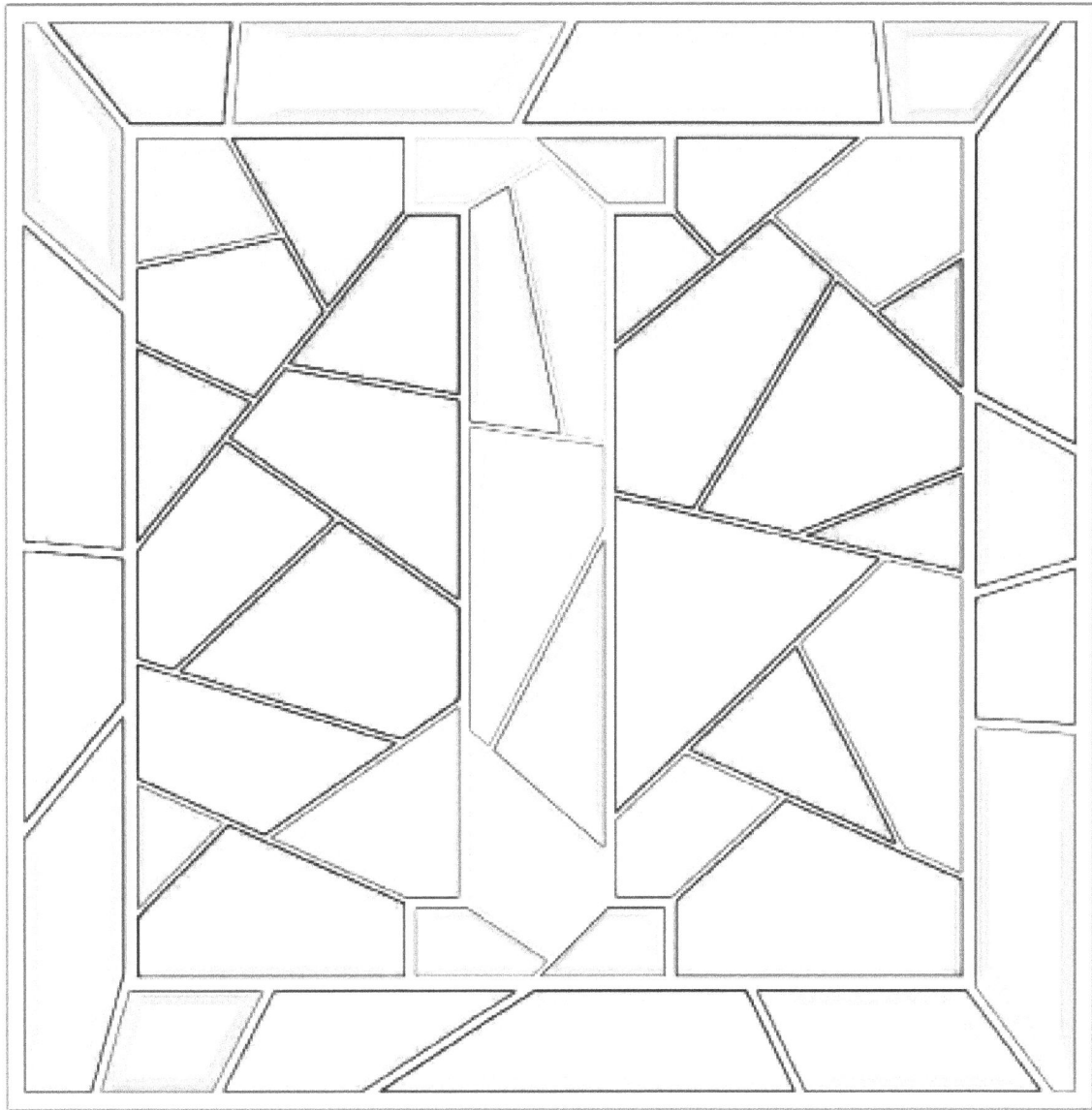

I is for
Immanuel

High Tide Publications, Inc.
1000 Bland Point
Deltaville, Virginia 23043
www.hightidepublications.com
First edition

ISBN: 978-1-945990-17-5

Graphic Arts and Illustrations: www.firebelliedfrog.com

I have immense appreciation for Jeanne Johansen, publisher, who has brought my Xavier to life. She gives us such delightful scenes of Angels at work and play. Her imaginative insight and clever artistry lets us peek beyond the clouds into celestial wonders

Her success as a publisher of excellence continues to be recognized in High Tide Publishing.

Joyce Carr Stedelbauer

HighTide
Publications, Inc.

Printed in the USA

Deltaville, Virginia

www.ingramcontent.com/pod-product-compliance
Lightning Source LLC
LaVergne TN
LVHW070835080426
835508LV00031B/3464